Continue Moving on in Life

First Edition: 2025

ISBN: 978-93-7335-526-9

Continue Moving on in Life

DON'T STOP MOVING

Layu Festus Praise

ACKNOWLEDGEMENT

First and foremost, I give all thanks to God for enduing and equipping me with the grace to write this book. I would also love to appreciate my family: my parents and my siblings who kept on encouraging and motivating me to be a better person each and every day. To my mentor, Mr. Elufowohan Oluwatobiloba, I deeply appreciate him for challenging my potentials by encouraging me do what my peers aren't doing to experience what they are striving to get and for bringing out the best in me - making sure my vision is well guided. And to Mr. Yomi Moses Daniel and Mr. Lateef Olusegun, thank you so much for being a strong support and a source of inspiration.

Dedication

I dedicate this book to every individual out there - both young and old - who need to understand that life is based on choice, which means the choices we make today is a determinant of our tomorrow.

FORWARD

Life is a journey marked by seasons of growth, setbacks, and breakthroughs. For many, the challenges along the way can feel like roadblocks that keep us from reaching our full potential when we lack the knowledge to live well or have someone who directs us. Yet, it is in these very moments of struggle that we find opportunities for transformation.

Continue Moving in Life is not just a book—it is a guide, a companion, and a source of inspiration for anyone who has ever felt stuck, uncertain, or overwhelmed by the weight of life's challenges.

I have had the privilege of mentoring Praise and witnessing his remarkable journey firsthand. Praise's story is not one of smooth sailing but one of courage, resilience, and faith. He has faced his share of trials—moments when giving up seemed easier than pushing forward. But instead of succumbing to the pressures of life, he chose a different path. He leaned into his faith, trusted God as his ultimate director, and discovered the power of authenticity and perseverance.

This book is a testament to the power of transformation. It is a reflection of Praise's personal growth and his desire to extend a helping hand to others navigating similar struggles. Through heartfelt stories, practical insights, and deeply rooted wisdom, Praise shares not only what he has learned but also how he has learned it. He reminds us that life's challenges, while difficult, are not insurmountable. With the right mindset, guidance, and trust in God, we can overcome any obstacle and step into the greatness we were created for.

This particular book is relevant for young people who feel like their dreams are slipping away or who believe they've hit a dead end. Yet, his message is one of hope. He demonstrates that no matter how miserable our circumstances may seem, there is always a way forward—one guided by purpose, fueled by determination, and anchored on faith.

As I read through these pages, I was reminded of the importance of mentorship and community. Praise's journey is one I am proud to have played a role in, but his success is a testament to his unwavering commitment to growth.

Mentorship is a partnership, a collaboration where both parties learn, grow, evolve and become. He has taken the lessons he received which might not be coning transformed them into a blueprint for others who wants to dare life also.

This book is more than advice; it is an invitation. An invitation to reflect on where you are and where you want to be.

This is a call to every reader to embrace their challenges, trust in God's plan, and take the next step toward their destiny.

Through this work, he has exemplified and revealed what it means to be a leader, a mentor, and a servant of God.

I knew our story will be told yet I am still awed in how well he has learned. Because of my position in his life I had to teach him the truth and open up about my struggles, sometimes doubts, and the moments when faith is the only anchor. That vulnerability is what makes this book so impactful—it is real, relatable, and deeply inspiring.

As you dive into Continue Moving in Life, I encourage you to approach it with an open heart and mind. Reflect on the wisdom shared, apply the lessons to your own journey, and allow yourself to be challenged and transformed. This book has the power to ignite a fire within you, to remind you that no matter how tough life gets, with God as your director, you can and will overcome.

To you Praise, I say this: I am immensely proud of you. Your courage to share your story and your commitment to helping others navigate their own paths is a testament to the person you have become.

This book is a gift to the world, and I am confident it will touch countless lives, offering hope, encouragement, and the reminder that we are all capable of moving forward, no matter the odds.

Dear reader, as you turn these pages, may you be reminded of the strength within you. May this book inspire you to embrace your journey, trust the process, and continue moving in life.

Oluwatobiloba Elufowohan.

Founder Invaders Global.

CONTENTS

INTRODUCTION

We all need to move on in life and one of the keys to doing this is to be determined. I think starting with one of the greatest experience I've ever had would help us all in understanding the main idea in this book. When I was in primary school, I was one of the best student, and of course, I had always received an award at the end of every session. Most of my peers then do envy me a lot; I was brilliant, intelligent and very bright. During classes, they would come to me and even doing coursework, some would ask me, how did you do that? As at that time the main support I had was my mum, who was only managing the little she had to take of her dear son.

I entered a new class - a new session, - only to discover that I couldn't understand what I was being taught. This happened when I was in grade 1. I was only able to stand out like I used to as a result of my mother's constant teachings - as she used to be an English Language teacher before establishing her business. Surprisingly, after few weeks, my academic performance started elevating.

Tomorrow is sure for you! But the way you manage your today is a determinant of the outcome of your tomorrow. Life is a continuous event, which is why as time goes on, we must keep moving. Though we never stop moving, but do you know where you are heading to? Is it the right or the wrong direction?

To continue moving on in life does not just mean to move but to move forward. That is, not looking back at the setbacks you once had in the past, but seeing a greater future ahead of you. You shouldn't stop moving because when you do, it brings back the past moments of dreadful experiences. You have to be determined within yourself that you are going to make it in life. ***A man who fails to plan, plans to fail - automatic failure***. Your determination shows that you have plans for the future since it is a determinant of your destination tomorrow. Since life is in progression, we also have to keep moving on (forward) as time waits for no one.

My mother, **Mrs. Oluchi Ezeh** has never lost hope for once. She would always say to us ***"I have the feeling and confidence that I can't be poor cause I am going to be successful. It's just a matter of time".*** At the slightest minute to being wailed down by any challenge, she would say those words; and it served as a motivator for me.

"Success comes as a result of determination; determination breeds success."

Chapter One
The Running Race

Every prize demands that you run a race. You getting a prize means you have done something no one in your field actually could do. Your determination tells what achievement you will make in life. You need to have a deep determination, so as to have a beautiful and motivating story to tell about your life accomplishments (achievements) in the nearest future. If I may ask, *"what should your determination be?"* Should it be for you to continue moving on, or end the non - motivating and non-captivating story there? Do you know that If you choose to end it there, it means you won't have any achievement or story to tell about your life? Yes, you won't! But when you choose to continue moving on, it means you are still looking forward to that great future of yours.

You can't run a race successfully without coming across obstacles. Before starting, you need to be determined within yourself that you will win it. More also, when running, face whatever obstacle that comes your way without looking back at the previous failures you had in the past because when you do, you'll surely get tired and weak to continue the race.

"The journey of life is not far, but your determination is a determinant of how far it will take you to get there". –

(My mentor- Mr. Elufowohan Oluwatobiloba)

The outcome of determination is achievement, and your achievement is what makes up a successful story. An instance was when I was faced with failure when I was in the ninth grade, to be precise. I realized that the race that I was to run doesn't only require hard work from reading and studying, but determination. I determined within myself that I was not going to fail any subject or score less than a fifty percent at the end of the session. Fortunately for me, I came out with flying colors. Not only that, I was also awarded the best student in my class. And why did it turn out to be like that? It's because I operated on the platform of determination in order to achieve my goal.

Before then, at the beginning of that session, first term to be precise, my performance declined, but I was still among the top ten. When I said my score went down, I meant that my score reduced from A to B. This reduction was actually because of the fear I had when two students who were twins got enrolled into the school. At first sight, I knew instantly that they were brilliant and of high intellects, but it turned out that only one was extremely intelligent while the other was an average student.

Every morning at 6: 39am, Kehinde was always seen reading till the assembly bell rang. I studied her all through the first three weeks of resumption and came to a conclusion that she was more brilliant than I. Due to Kehinde's character, which I would consider as proudness, I was unable to relate with her because she would always snub me for asking questions regarding any coursework. On the other hand, I had my best friend. Honestly speaking, he was more good at solving mathematical problems and some science courses than anyone else in my class even though his future ambition was to be an accountant. Looking at both of them, I lost focus; started considering myself a failure. Anxiety and fear set in. I became pessimistic about everything I did at school. Suddenly, at the end of the mid term test, I got third place in every subject. Even some of my teachers were very surprised about it. I got home at the end of the term only to show my mum that I took the third position.

During the holiday, I said to myself *"Festus, I will be the first this time around"*. School resumed and coursework started, and I remember vividly that every single day I would say those words to myself. With time I became much more confident of my success. I started scoring high in most subjects and that was how I eventually became the first and also the best student of my set.

One of the scriptural examples of men who operated on this very

platform is Jesus. According to **Revelation 5: 2-5, it says:**

And I saw a strong angel proclaiming with a loud voice, who is able to open the book and to loose the seals thereof?

And no man in heaven, nor in earth, neither under the earth, was able to open the book, neither to look thereon.

And I wept much, because no man was found worthy to open

and to read the book, neither to look thereon.

And one of the elders saith unto me. Weep not; behold the lion of the tribe of Judah, the root of David, hath prevailed to open the

book, to loose the seven seals thereof.

From that scripture, I realized that Jesus was only able to open the book and save the world from sin by sharing his blood on the cross for our salvation and redemption because He was determined.

Revelation 5: 7 says;

"And he came and took the book out of the hand of Him that sat upon the throne".

While Jesus was on the mission to redeem us, He also came across many challenges. He was tested, tempted, accused, beaten, brutalized, criticized, and laid down on the cross till his death. He kept on running the race because He knew there was something He would achieve at the end of it all.

A person who doesn't pass through temptation, trials, and obstacles is not yet a Christian. Christianity means Christ like! If Jesus could face all these, why won't we? A man who is not determined is not a Christian, but a believer; he only believes Jesus is Lord, heaven is real and that it is mandatory for him to attend services every Sunday, but doesn't have what it takes to get there. Becoming a Christian means to be determined to face war. Moreover, a race is not always declared finished until you run to the finish line, and not just that, but being the Frontier (the first runner up).

Chapter Two

In Every Scar Is A Star.

To begin, I'd love to let you know that in every scar is a star, and there's no star without a scar. This is one of the famous quote of my father in the Lord, the founder of Living Faith Church, Bishop David O. Oyedepo.

"In every scar is a star, and there's no star without a scar"

-Bishop David O. Oyedepo.

"You have to do what others are not doing to be on top"

– Elufowohan Oluwatobiloba (My mentor).

To be at the top, there are a lot of sacrifices you have to make. Success does not just come to us; it comes along with a sacrifice you have to make. There's no successful man on earth who did not sacrifice one thing or the other, most especially the Men of God. For example, we have **Bishop David Oyedepo, Prophet TB Joshua, and Dr. Ben Carson (My medical mentor).** We will be examining these three reputable figures in the society and how they were able to get to where they are today.

Bishop David Oyedepo: Papa (as we call him) had to sacrifice a lot to be where he is today. The commission, Living Faith Church Worldwide was built on the platform of sacrifice and dedication to kingdom service. He sacrificed the whole of himself to God. He sacrificed his time and space to God. He fasted, prayed, and this is a man who always listens to God, making the things of God his first priority. There was a time he mentioned it in church that he asked mama to sign a contract which explains that whatever mission God sends him on, even though it would cost his life, would she still marry him? He is a man who is committed to reading and never stops reading.

Another instance was when he travelled out of the country, and got back home only to show Mama the loads of books he bought since he had promised her that he was going to buy things for her. I think this should answer the question why Bishop David Oyedepo is very knowledgeable. There was a time a man went to his house, entered into his library, and met him reading. Seeing a lot of books, the man was so surprised to the extent that he could not comprehend what he saw.

One more thing is his untiring Kingdom service to God. His main focus has always been ***Mathew 6: 33 which says " Seek ye first the kingdom of God and his righteousness, and all other things shall be added unto you".*** He also mentioned this scripture to be one of the tools that has triggered the growth of the church from being a fivemember congregation to a fifty thousand, from national to international recognition.

Prophet TB Joshua: Prophet TB Joshua, the founder of Synagogue Church of All Nations, had always put God first in spite of the challenges he faced in the past, even until he died in 2021. He fasted and prayed earnestly and mostly on the mountain. He did Charity which is a way of expressing our love to God. He was a man of Charity! Don't just think he woke up one day and started doing miracles as a result of the gift of God in him. He fasted and prayed before he could ever become who he is today.

Dr. Benson Carson: Dr. Carson, a neurosurgeon, neuro- oncologist, and a pediatric surgeon, mentioned in one of his books titled "Gifted Hands" that he had to start watching only three TV programs and also read two books every week as instructed by his mother. He said it was not convenient, and that he could have also lied about doing them, but he didn't want to disobey his mother. He did it out of inconvenience, and that's what a sacrifice is. He could have joined the football team and played all through the day, but he never did! He was made to do what others were not doing. Today, he is well known as the first Neurosurgeon to separate the Siamese twins who were joined together by a very vital vein known as the Superior Sagittal Sinus. A type of conjoined twins also known as Occipital craniopagus twins, which had never been successfully separated with both surviving.

Bishop Benson Idahosa: Bishop Benson Idahosa, who is also known as the father of Pentecostalism. He grew up in a society - as a native of Benin state - where witches determine who should live or not. A society that when a witch tells a person is going to die at 2:00 in the afternoon, such person will. Benson Idahosa grew up in a family where his father hated him all because of his health status. He went through a lot of difficult times. He did a lot of miracles and raised eight dead people before his death at the age of 59 years in 1997. One of his missions was to reach everybody about Christ. He was a man of prayer. A man who never gave up on praying and preaching the gospel. He reached out to over 135 countries, preaching the gospel, in which most were uninvited visits. I will undoubtedly say that the determination to fulfill God's assignment over his life and his prayerful lifestyle is one of the pillars behind his successful story.

Listen, life operates on the principle of give and take, while on what platform you give determines your success or outcome in life. That is to get something, you will need to also give; It involves what I call the Sacrificial – Success Transaction.

Jesus had to starve in order to be empowered towards the reason of His coming. (**Luke 4:2**)

Being forty days tempted of the devil, In those days He did eat nothing. - ***Luke 5:3 (Paraphrased)***

He did not eat anything for a whole forty days, and at the same time, He was tempted all through those days by the devil. But at the end of it all, His mission on earth started because He was empowered. I know some would say, ***"That was Jesus and why would you compare us to Him?"*** But let me tell you, maybe you might have forgotten that Jesus came into this world in flesh; He was a human being like us. He sacrificed his hunger and thirst so that you and I might be saved. Jesus said in ***Luke 22: 36 "For I say unto you, that this that is written must be accomplished in me…"***. Why don't we take that step? Why can't we make sure that that which has been written concerning us, our purpose in life which is in His word must be accomplished? For our redemption, He had to endure all the suffering. For Christ knowing what was set before Him, endured the cross so that we might be saved (**Paraphrased**) – **Hebrews 22:2**.

As an individual, if you don't want to take risks, you can't make it. You should be ready to face challenges! All things are easy to get except you're not ready to face what it takes to get it. All through my secondary school days (high school), I was among the top students because I chose to have a scar, and what was the scar? Taking the time to study and pray instead of playing football, going out with friends, watching movies, and every other thing that we derive pleasure from. I studied, attended services and choir rehearsals, went to school, listened to instructions, prayed while my mates are having a nice time together. I am not saying I don't have fun. I joke, play with friends, watch movies, but not all the time. In fact, when I told a colleague of mine all that I do, she said to me, "you have good management skills", which I never even had because I'm the kind of person who doesn't stick to the time table; the time and activities will surely get mixed up. There was a time when I was in senior high school, that I did not watch TV for a whole term. It was after my exams that I became interested. There was TV but no one was interested in watching any. Instead of watching TV, my siblings would rather play. I also remember there was a time I actually did watch a lot, and that was when I was in junior high school.

Don't think I was too serious. No! I wasn't but one thing I'm sure I never did was to make many friends. Just recently, a sister of mine asked if I have been able to make new friends in my new residence. Moreover, I can hardly make friends, The reason is because I try to do things differently from the way others do and that might make us incompatible. Before I could call you a best friend, then it means I have seen something that amazes me about you. It means our character and attitude is somehow alike.

Chapter Three

The Power Of Hope, Faith And Love.

Hope signifies the expectation of an event to occur. It is having the assurance of the slightest possibility of an event to occur. According to scriptures, hope is among the three main principles (Faith, Love, and Hope) Christians are meant to operate on. For more understanding of this great virtue, I will be explaining a little about how my mentor found hope in his future.

I remember writing this same story when I was applying to Hope college which is situated in Holland, USA. After sending in my application, I decided to apply for the college most prestigious scholarship known as **"Hope Forward"**. During the process of my application, I was asked to write an essay of over 1200 words on the virtue **"Hope"**. Explaining the importance of finding hope in hopeless situations, using mentors or role models as a case study. So, I decided to use my mentor's real life story. Writing my scholarship essay, I wrote as thus;

- *At Hope, It is believed that the biggest problems in the world isn't that there are problems, but that there's no hope in our ability to resolve these problems. I strongly believe this ideology to be true. Though faith will be tested but the base of all solutions is holding unto God because all the virtues we have will also be tested. I'd love to speak about the academic life of my mentor, how he brought hope to an area of hopelessness in his life, community, and the world at large. More also, I will be giving emphasis on what I learnt from him, how he influenced who I am today, and how he motivated me to spread hope to the world.*

  He once told me that we are not shortsighted to see that there are big problems around us, but what there is, is not the issue about the problem, but the mind we have to solve the problem. Most people don't normally see the solutions to problems while the best way to make it in life is when there are problems, and yet we don't want to face them, but want to make it in life. Even as recorded in the Bible, Jesus had to go through some challenges in order to solve something.

  It all began in 2015, when my mentor had just finished high school. There was no hope, assurance or light that he was going to attend a university. No one was concerned about him and initially, he has never lived with his parents, but grandparents instead. He had to involve himself in all jobs to be able to get to where he is today. There was a time he had an issue of financial insecurity and opted out for a way to save himself from stealing or doing anything that would bring shame to anyone.

Before then, at a point in his life while he was still in high school, he had to sell fruits, take it to school, and sell each at the rate of five naira which is significantly less than a dollar in today's equivalent. He leaves the house by six in the morning and returns back home six in the evening, having worked all day. In fact, he had to do some odd jobs which included working as a service boy, repairing his colleagues' worn out shoes and sandals; as he used to be a cobbler. He felt there was no light anywhere at all and the only thing that kept him hoping for a better future was his strong belief in Christ. He studied the word of God and there he found out that there are so many good things that would come into his life if only he could wait and stay with Him(God). He believed every single word he found in the scripture. Most times, while thinking over what to do, inspiration comes and things get done instantly. With that, he had a very high expectation that he was eventually going to make it in spite of everything.

After high school graduation, no one was ready to take the responsibility of sending him to the university. Nevertheless, he opted in for Joint Admission and Matriculation Board Examination which is also known as "JAMB", an aptitude test for entry into universities in Nigeria. To be able to pay his fees to write this examination, he sold chips. He wrote the examination and passed, but there was no money to pay for his admission even though he would be given one. After finishing the first examination which was his first attempt, he realized that if he should stop there, his life would remain miserable, and no one would hear of his story and be motivated to do something.

Later on, he decided within himself that he was not going to attend any tutorial in order to write and pass the examination the second time, but would rather study it on his own and go there to teach them. In the process of teaching at tutorial classes, he gained a lot. He sat for the examination, passed, but unfortunately, he was sided with just 0.1 mark in the university's main examination.

Basically because of those that are behind him and his parents whom he never wanted to end up the same way they ended up, he had to do something about it by working on himself and believing even when everything seems odd. He hoped in his problems that in his problems, there are solutions. Moreover, when there is a problem, all we need to do is to keep the struggle hopefully.

Sometimes it will cost a lot of things, but better still, take it than to lose a generation over a simple step you would have taken to ease everything. With this, it brought to him and to the hopeless that no matter how or where you're heading to, it's just a pastime to help strengthen, build, and equip you for what is going to happen in the nearest future. Fortunately, at the end of it all, he got admission to study at one of the best universities in Nigeria (University of Ibadan, UI). Through the challenges he passed through academically, he now understands what leadership and financial ability is all about.

Under his mentorship, I realized that without problems one can never be successful. The way we attend to challenges in life determines how far we would go in life. He taught me to always embrace difficulties and challenges because it is out of it I am going to get a solution. I learnt to always be ready to encounter problems. There was a time I wrote an examination and passed well and what he told me was, ***"Don't think you have done the best yet because there is still more to be done".***

Looking back at who I am today and will be in the future, his effort and impact is significantly recognized. He made me understand that things will not always work out the way we want it to. I realized that to be successful, I need to take responsibility. Since he taught me the difference between the right and correct thing, I've made it my lifestyle and have always been watching out for the right thing, the right decisions to make and the right opportunities to opt in. He gave me the reason to believe there's no hard subject, course or examination, and that the only thing we often consider is the correct and not the right thing instead.

The motivation to bring hope to the world is one vital instrument of success stories. He motivated me to bring hope to the world via my virtues, morals, and academic excellence by letting me know that everyone is a solution to a particular problem.

It's not about the problem itself but it is the perspective of the problem that actually determines how well a solution can be given. More also, if you're faced with a challenge, just know it is for three things which includes to keep you equipped, to make you realize that without God you are nothing, and also to make those behind you realize the God's perspective over your life.

– **Elufowohan Oluwatobiloba** (**Layu Festus Praise**).

I'm sorry I have to keep you going through all those details, but it's just that I can't skip a part of it because every single sentence has very vital information to tell you about the virtue **"Hope".** Summarizing everything, I have written, it is clear that my mentor believes that there's always a solution to every problem we encounter in life and that this is what makes us successful in life.

Secondly, we have faith, which is the substance of things hoped for and the evidence of things not seen (**Hebrews 11:1 – 3**). Faith is the assurance of things we hope to have or get. Things we can't see, but hope for it. It is important we note that faith does not just start, it is a gradual process (**Romans 10:10**). I remember the story of a man who doesn't have a car, but planned to purchase one with the zero naira he had in his account. He got to where he was to buy the car, picked his preferred one, and told the manager he was going to come and pick it up the next day. This man knew he had nothing, but he believed he would get one. He went back the next day and on getting there, he met a rich man who wanted to buy the exact car he chose the previous day. Immediately he told the rich man that it was his preferred car. Surprisingly, the rich man said *"ok, let me pick this and you pick that one, don't worry, I will settle all the bills"*. And that was how this man got his own car with zero naira in his account.

Faith is expecting what seems unbelievable to others. It is believing the unbelievable and unworkable by human mentality. This is something I have tried several times and at the same time gotten good results. Faith does not work when you have doubts because it is actually the opposite. Faith has the capacity to make the impossible come into existence.

Faith does not happen by proclaiming that you have it. Show me your faith and I will show you my work. Faith without Work is Fake. It requires a process which is putting it to work. The Scripture says in ***Romans 8: 18 "So then faith cometh by hearing and hearing by the word of God"(KJV)***. I really love the Amplified Version of this verse which says;

> ***So faith comes from hearing [what is told], and what is heard comes by the [preaching of the] message concerning Christ. – Romans 10:17(AMP).***

From the above scripture, it is evident that to build up our faith we have to hear and not just that but hearing (present continuous tense) the word of God regularly. We have to continue hearing the word of God either by studying His Word or by the preaching of the Word.

Faith keeps us moving; it aids continuous movement and progress in life. With God, all things are possible only when you believe. For instance, there was this movie I watched that featured a village king who had a God sent (messenger) in his palace. A messenger who was sent to liberate the people of the village from the wicked hand of the seven sucking demons. On a particular day, the king became very afraid that his chiefs would do something evil to the man of God that was in his palace. And after the man of God had raised his dead son, the king and his household all gave their lives to Christ, which was what made his chiefs furious. Thereafter the man of God started preaching to the king and his household, telling them about Jesus and the wonders He does. During one of the Bible study hours, this young man read a part of the scriptures in Psalm which says ***"When my enemies come against me, they will all stumble"***. After hearing this, the king became so drunk with that verse, and he believed that no matter the circumstances around him, he would overcome his enemies.

Another instance was when Peter saw Jesus walking on the sea. He also tried it, but at a particular time he doubted, thinking he would fall and immediately he began to sink. And what does that tell us? It tells us that faith keeps us moving no matter the economic status of the world, but at a second of doubt, movement stops.

The third instance is the story of Abraham. Abraham kept on believing every single word God spoke to him. Remember the time God asked him to sacrifice his only son, which he did without doubting. He kept on moving because He believed whatever God does is 'Good'.

The third is Love. Love is the greatest commandment ever. It is also the greatest of the three principal forces that defines the destiny of a believer. ***1 Corinthians 2: 9 – 10 says " But as it is written; what eyes hath not***

seen, nor ears heard, neither have entered into the heart of man, the things which God hath prepared for them that love him". I remember vividly when I first saw this verse in the Bible was when one of my elder brothers in church was teaching me about the different types of voices(spiritual) and our inheritance in Christ via our love for God. After seeing it, I couldn't but pounder on it every single second. And why was that? It's because our love for God opens up possibilities. Look at the extent of the excess blessing that will be bestowed on us on the platform of our love for God – what eyes hath not seen, what the world have never experienced, what the world have never heard, witnessed nor thought of all come to us on the platform of love.

When you love God, you should always expect possibilities. Love for God stirs up a man's faith to continue moving on in spite of his surrounding circumstances; optimism set in. It makes our spirit man robust to overcome every challenge in life and keep us moving. We can only continue moving on if we choose to love God – as love is a choice – by studying, thinking, doing the word, and praying consistently (**Psalm 61: 1-3**). Remember faith works by love (**Hebrews 11: 17-29**).

Another aspect of love is loving your neighbors. The scripture says love your neighbor as yourself (The second is like the first). And now abideth faith, hope, charity (love), these three; but the greatest of these is

Charity (**1 Corinthians 13: 13**). Though I speak in tongues, I have the gift of prophecy, understand all mysteries, and all knowledge and even have a strong faith, and have not charity, I am nothing – paraphrased (**1 Corinthians 1&2**). Via our love for God, we become a mobile solution provider (**Mark 10: 27**).

Loving your neighbor as yourself also explains what is called **"Being Nice"**. According to Dr. Benson Carson, a renowned neurosurgeon, being nice means not talking about other people behind their backs or not talking about people in front of their backs *(If you see somebody struggling with something, help him or her with it)*. Put yourself in their shoes before you begin to criticize. An instance he explained is if the elevator door is open and there is only one space left, let someone else get on. When you're driving your car and someone puts a blinker on, don't speed up, slow down and let them in, and in terms of speaking to people; when you get in an elevator. 'Good morning'. This is no doubt a way of being nice (showing love) to others in the family, neighborhood, community, among our peers and fellow workers.

The scripture also recorded when Jesus said to us *'do unto others as you would also have others do unto you'*. Our love for God puts Him in our situation; It calls for God's presence.***1 John 4:19 – 21 says;***

v19. "We love Him, because He first loved us.

> ***v20. If a man says, I love God and hateth his brother, he is a liar: for he that loveth not his brother whom he hath seen, how can he love God whom he hath not seen?***
>
> ***v21. And this commandment we have from him. That he who loveth God love his brother also".***

Another instance was when Jesus said in **John 13:14** that ***"A new commandment I give unto you. That ye love one another; as I have loved you, that ye also may love one another"***. I'd love to let you know that when you speak about your fellows behind their backs, your progress in life becomes terminated. You should be able to correct them. Tell them politely that what they have done is wrong and also give possible solutions to it because this in another way gives you the opportunity to be able to overcome those failures and continue moving on when they get to you. But when you criticize and blame others for things they have done behind their back, you automatically terminate the BIG PICTURE of yourself.

Chapter Four

Patience: Key To Success

Many lives have been cut short due to their inability to endure. Patience pays a lot. As I write, I just wonder why we call sick people who lay in bed at the hospital 'patient', and then this word came through my mind that *"it's because they're patient enough to receive treatment without turning back till they get better"*. These people wait patiently in bed, expecting that very soon they will be fine and will go back to their families. They endure a lot in the process of staying as a patient patiently in bed. That's not the real thing, but all I'm trying to let us know is what it is to endure. Hoping actually requires being patient enough to wait on God.

Yes, we encounter a lot of challenges in our lives, but patience can really make those years of suffering a lifetime breakthrough. Being patient means waiting on God; enduring in spite of the circumstances around us. It is a very vital virtue we need to have when running the race of life; It takes patience to be successful in life.

Patience makes a believer wealthy (in the sense of all round rest). Through **Hebrews 12: 2**, we are made to understand that there are a lot of benefits allotted to us when we wait patiently on God. Looking unto Jesus the author and finisher of our faith; who for the joy that was set before Him endured the cross, despising the same, and is set down at the right hand of the throne of God. For the 'Joy' that was set before Christ, He endured the cross. He didn't consider the pain He would go through, but He focused on his targeted mission to bring salvation back to mankind – for our redemption – so as to obtain the promise.

Why do we encounter challenges?

Overcoming challenges turns our poverty into prosperity. We can only access the promise when we endure, and there's no endurance until there's a challenge. We encounter them because of the following reasons:

TO OBTAIN THE PROMISE

We gain access to the promise of God through faith and patience. ***Hebrews 6: 24 – 15 says "Saying, surely***

blessing I will bless thee and multiplying I will multiply thee. And so after he had patiently endured, he obtained the promise". If you really paid attention to that verse, you would see that he had waited patiently before he could obtain the promise. Meaning patience is very vital in obtaining the promise of God. Abraham waited patiently. I'm sure in the case of Abraham, many would have abused, mocked, and even condemned him, but he still endured all and remained steadfast in faith. He didn't faint, instead he kept on believing. Rest in the Lord, and wait patiently for Him (**Psalm 37: 7**). King David said I waited patiently for the Lord; and he inclined unto me, and heard my cry. ***Ecclesiastes 8: 9, also says 'Better is the end of a thing than the beginning thereof and the patient in spirit is better than the proud heart'.***

Since we now know that better is the end of a thing than the beginning, why can't we remain patient? There's no reason why we shouldn't wait on God except if we want to remain a proud entity - accessing the end at the beginning. Don't rush, wait because your story will soon change.

FOR OUR SELF DEVELOPMENT.

Most times the challenges we encounter in life helps us to build ourselves not only in the faith, but spirituality as well. We encounter challenges so that we can learn to be patient enough. We should know that every problem we find ourselves is a test of time.

I realized that Christians pray the most when they're in a terrible condition. We should understand that praying only when we have problems does not move God, instead we should just keep on praying the more. For instance, you have not been praying for the past three months neither have you been reading your Bible nor attending church services, but because you now have a debt to pay, you've started praying, and speaking those words to God. Your relationship with God today is what makes you prepared for future circumstances. You should start preparing for that problem now and not when it comes. And not only so, but we glory in tribulation also, knowing that tribulation worketh patience; And patience, experience; and experience, hope (**Romans 5: 3 – 4**). If we don't wait patiently on God even in our current situations, we won't have any story to tell nor will anybody be motivated by our story.

TO LEARN TO BE PATIENT.

Naturally, if we don't encounter problems, we would never learn to be patient. It requires patience to get the better part of an event or a thing. Patience in terms of conflict or issue can also be termed as being nice. When someone says a very annoying word to you, instead of doing the same, why don't you just hold back your anger (calm your nerves). The best answer for a fool is to be silent. Though, sometimes you have to let the fool know he's behaving like one at the moment, but it requires you sieving your words right before speaking.

Mr. Femi Ayanbadejo will always say, *"You should learn to sieve your words, including your thoughts, what you hear, and even what you see, before saying anything"*. Most times (not all the time) silence makes a fool realize that he is wrong while some people might say that you're likewise foolish or stupid for keeping quiet. In this case, the Holy Spirit will be of great help. When you have the Holy Spirit in you, you will learn to do the right thing at the right time. See also: **Eccl 7:10, I Thess 5: 4, Heb 6:15, Psalm 37:7, Psalm 41:1, James 1:2 – 4,12 – 14, 5:17, Heb 19:36.**

HOW TO BE PATIENT (IN THE JOURNEY OF LIFE).

To enhance continuous movement, you need to do the following which we will be examining from **Hebrews 12:1 – 3.**

> ***Vs 1. Wherefore, seeing we also are compassed about with so great a cloud of witnesses, let us lay aside every weight, and the sin which doth so easily beset us; and let us run with patience the race that is set before us.***
>
> ***Vs 2. Looking into Jesus the author and finisher of our faith, who for the joy that was set before him endured the cross, despising the Shame, and is set down at the right hand of God.***

Vs 3. For consider him that endured such contradiction of sinners against himself, lest ye be weary and faint in your minds – Hebrews 12:1 – 3

BE FOCUSED.

Great fortune comes as a result of being focused. Focus means laying aside every weight (concentrating) thereby enabling us to run the race that is set before us. Impatience makes an athlete disqualified from running a race. When you become impatient, you tend to shift your focus towards another thing. Honestly, I've heard this word several times and still hear them every single day of my life. Some may not say it directly to me, but I can tell that's the actual message my mentor, colleagues and family are trying to pass across to me.

SET YOUR AFFECTION ON THINGS ABOVE.

Colossians 2:3 & 3:3 was what took me to my study destination. I got this scripture while I was praying, asking God what he had to say concerning my current situation.

"In whom are hid all the treasures of wisdom and knowledge" – Col 2:3

"Set your affection on things above, not on things on the earth" – Col 3:2

Make God your first priority in life and not just that, but also seek for his righteousness (**Matt. 6:33**), (**1 Cor.**

2:9 – 10) because sin can also hinder answers to our prayers. You have to put away those sinful acts before you can become who God wants you to be. Most people only seek God first, forgetting the part that says **"righteousness"**. Before now, I was also among that set of people, but the only difference was that I knew about it and also understood what it means but I have never given much attention to it whenever I speak to people using that scripture, even as a house fellowship leader in my church. Not until one of my brothers in church came to me on a particular Sunday during service, sat beside me at the choir seat and said to me, 'do you know most people only seek God's kingdom through kingdom service but forget about his righteousness, which is one of the main reason why most workers in the church don't see result as they ought to.

DON'T CONSIDER THE SHAME, BUT WATCH OUT FOR THE BENEFITS (RESULTS)

According to verse two of **Hebrews Chapter 12**, it is evident that Jesus never considered the shame but the joy that was set before Him. He endured the cross. He was mocked, beaten, spotted on, and likewise he was also given a sour drink. He didn't consider all the pain, not at all any. I never gave serious attention to the shame I would face when I had a result I never wanted nor expected, instead I stepped up and faced reality. Once you consider the shame, you might never be able to accomplish your goals anymore because your focus has already been shifted.

My aunt will always say that When you fall, all you need to do is to stand up immediately and not asking God why. Why not use that period to stand up and improve on yourself rather than asking why?

DON'T BE WEARY (CONTROL YOUR MIND).

My mentor (Mr. Elufowohan Oluwatobiloba) always makes this statement that who you think you are is a determinant of who you'll be in the future. Your perspective about yourself affects your outcome in life. You can't have a poor mentality and still aim high. It's not possible. If your mentality is that you can never be wealthy, then you'll never be. You should start proclaiming good things to yourself. The scripture says, as a man thinketh in his heart, so is he. Meaning your thought is a reflection of yourself. What you think about yourself is who you really are. Your thoughts determine the kind of trophy life would award to you. Your thought is what makes you; it is the reflection of your personality – who you are. This is one of the things I would be emphasizing on in my next book.

You should be able to sieve your thoughts right because if you don't, your thoughts will eventually end up sieving you – Mr. Ayanbadejo Oluwafemi.

CHAPTER FIVE

RESPONSIBILITY: THE PRICE OF GREATNESS

This is more of real life encounters because I will be explaining some vital points using real life stories. I will be taking us through a lot of details in this chapter. However, I would love you to be very attentive to the given details.

Applying to Universities Abroad

Now listen, this is where the main point is. I started applying to colleges in the Unites States right from grade 12, but I had to stop since they were all requesting WASSCE results which I hadn't written yet then. Few months later, I finished my WASSCE exam and expected A parallel, but unfortunately for me I got had a pass in mathematics. I was devastated after seeing my result. I was so ashamed to the extent that I couldn't tell my colleagues and juniors in school whom I taught mathematics, chemistry and physics because while I was in my final year in high school, I taught the grade eleven students chemistry tutorials for a whole term due to the absence of the subject teacher in the school.

Nevertheless, I never gave up. I continued the journey by attending a program where I was taught SAT, TOEFL, IELTS lessons and also how to go about studying in the US on scholarship. During the program, I also did a diploma course in Public Relations. After the program, I decided to write the SAT exam since my tutor said there's still a chance of gaining admission even with the pass mark I had and if I could also put more effort in my essays. Unfortunately, I couldn't write the exam because of an issue I had during my registration and since most schools had the test optional policy, I opted in for it. Even with that, I never told anyone aside from my family and mentor who knew I didn't write the examination and because of that, there was no way anyone could have helped me with my college application. So, I had to do it all by myself in order not to be discouraged by anyone, that with my result and no standardized test, admission was impossible.

Nobody taught me how to apply to colleges and universities in the US nor did anyone help me through my application period. I did it all by myself. I prayed, engaged in kingdom service. And after several weeks of waiting for admission decisions in the early decision, and early action poll, all I got from the schools were rejection letters. I applied to Hope college, University of Pennsylvania, DePaul University, University of Miami, and some other colleges. I know you would say, bro Festus, all these schools are top schools not to even talk of UPenn which is an ivy league. How do you expect them to give you an admission? But listen, I knew, but I applied since I had explained the reason behind the pass mark I had in mathematics and with my transcripts and recommendation letters which were excellent. I knew these were top schools, but I had faith that if God has really destined me to be in one of those schools, surely it will happen. I remembered what my mum said to me the next morning after the SAT registration deadline. She said 'don't be discouraged, God might not even want you to do these examinations in order for you to gain admission. In fact, you might do them and still not gain admission. Funnily enough, you know you might not even do any to gain an admission'. My mentor also had a lot to say about that too and he encouraged me to start praying for an hour everyday. And he would also send me books to read every month.

I didn't stop applying to universities outside Nigeria nor did I apply to any in Nigeria because I knew what the big picture holds for me. I had a lot of sleepless nights writing essays and applying to colleges, and it was during that period I realized I was a good essayist.

After three schools sent me rejection letters during the early decision period, I decided I was going to rewrite WASSCE and JAMB, then apply to Covenant or Landmark university to study biochemistry through the university's scholarship, and thereafter, I would go to the United States to further my studies. With that in mind, I registered for WASSCE, but I eventually did not write the exam because I gained admission before the examination start date.

At the beginning of last year, I decided to write out my goals for the year and among them I listed my admission along with a scholarship. I started praying for 30 minutes everyday, but my mentor asked me to add 30 more minutes to it, making it an hour everyday. I started it, but I wasn't a hundred percent consistent.

Few months later, I became very depressed and told God I wanted to hear him speak to me concerning the situation my family was experiencing. So, I stopped asking God I want this and that, and levelled up to asking Him What He was trying to say to me through the challenges. While praying, two scriptures dropped in my mind which are **Col 2:3 and Col 3:2.** The first was a question while the other was an answer to the first question.

In whom are hid all the treasures of wisdom and Knowledge

– Col 2:3

Set your affection on things above, not on things on the earth

- Col 3:2

Few days later, I was in my mother's room discussing with her when my phone notification turned on, then I read ***"an update has been made to your application"***. After seeing this, I checked my email and read the message from an A+ elite university in India which says I have been admitted into their biochemistry program with a 50% scholarship which is less than two thousand dollars. Moreover, the actual tuition was affordable for an international student like me, so I started preparing and asking questions from my admission counselor about the necessary things that needed to be done.

A week after, I was sent another acceptance letter from Lees McRae College, North Carolina, but the issue there was that I had to contribute more to my total cost of attendance. Though I pleaded, the school, the college was small, so they couldn't afford more than what they had given to me.

However, since Lees McRae College was not affordable for me, I decided to put in more effort in my application to other colleges. I applied for their Full Tuition Scholarships, wrote essays and also created my resume. And as for one of them, I was selected for the next stage as a finalist and also scheduled an interview which is the last stage of the scholarship application. No one was there to help me except God and the Holy spirit. I did the interview and the interviewer was so impressed by me and I guess that was the reason why I was persuaded with a prestigious scholarship. Though I was not given the full tuition scholarship which I guess is because other finalists had a better application profile than I did.

When I was sent my admission letter with my financial aid package, I couldn't stop wondering and giving thanks to God almighty.

Few weeks later another one came, and that was how they kept coming, but the amazing thing here is that I got admitted to more than twenty – five universities in three different countries without a standardized test.

A friend of Mine

A friend of mine taught me that responsibility is really the basis of every man's success in life. This is a young teenager who never sits idle for a moment. A time spent without doing something productive stresses her. At a very young age, she started affiliate marketing, Amazon KDP and digital marketing not because she wanted money, but because she knew she had to take a step if truly she wants to make it in life. In the seventh chapter, I would be explaining about positive thinking and words of affirmation. I made it the seventh chapter because it is very important that we understand that confession without profession results in depression.

My Mentor

Remember the story of my mentor who found hope in hopeless situations in order to achieve his purpose in life. ***"You need to do what nobody else is doing to get a result different from what others are getting".*** He had no one to take care of him, but he knew where he was going to, so he acted on his faith by taking responsibility. This is a man who never plays with his prayer time. He once told me 'Praise you need to understand that it requires you doing what others aren't doing to achieve God's purpose over your life. He also made this statement "It's a different thing to discover purpose and another to fulfill purpose. It takes responsibility to achieve purpose. A man who has discovered purpose but has no vision towards fulfilling it is just as useless as a mad man who doesn't know his next destination. Faith without work is dead. You believe you're going to be a great architect in the future, yet you sit idle doing nothing towards achieving it.

Chapter Six

Understanding God's Personality

This chapter is manned to expose us to the true expression of God's act. ***John 11: 1-3 says, "In the beginning was the Word and the Word was with God and the Word was God..... The same was in the beginning with God......All things are made by Him; and without Him was anything made that was made". (KJV).***

Sometimes people tag God wicked because they've somehow been through one or two things or let me use the word "afflicted". By doing so, they are unable to really understand the personality of God and His act. I have also experienced this before and in this chapter I will be giving instances so as to have an insight about God's personality and His act that whatsoever He does is always good. (Genesis 1:33). Some believers don't even serve God the way they are supposed to because they assume that God is wicked. I'm not only addressing this to the Christians, but to every other person because God is good and all the time......The Lord is good. We usually consider our own plight neglecting what God has to say about it. Like we all know that prayer is a two-way communication between God and man, which means in prayer, there's a caller and a receiver, but it's so complicated now that we only complain. Have we forgotten that He knows what you're facing, what you're going through….He knows all, do instead of just complaining, why don't you ask Him what He's trying to say to you. He's your father…..He would answer you as far as you ask with desperation, an expectant and an open heart.

We complain a lot in prayer telling God, I want a car, I want my own husband, I want to by a TV, I need a phone, I want to travel abroad, I need money….and so on. Let me tell you something. *Spiritual things give you access to material things with ease*. So why not go for the spiritual. King Solomon told God he wanted divine wisdom to be able to lead the people. If most of us were asked the same question God asked King Solomon, I'm sure we would have requested material things. But because King Solomon requested for the spiritual things, God gave him all other things. Have you forgotten what the Bible says in ***Matthew 6:33. It says "But seek ye first the kingdom of God and His righteous***

and all other things shall be added unto you".. The scripture did not only speak about kingdom service, it also made us understand that we have to walk in God's way. In fact for you to know what would be added unto us if we do that, an example of it is in ***1 Corinthians 2:9 which says "For what eyes have not seen, nor ears have heard not has it entered into the heart of man are those things which the Lord has prepared for those who love those who love Him" (Paraphrased)***. Remember what God said in Deuteronomy chapter 28. That if you shall obey and serve Him, you shall spend your days in prosperity and your years in pleasures (Paraphrased).

God's act supersedes man's act. ***"For my ways are higher than your ways and my thoughts higher than yours (For my thoughts are not your thoughts, neither are your ways my ways, saith the Lord) (Isaiah 55: 8-9)-Paraphrased***. I think it's high time we erase this mentality that we think the same way God does because we are made in his image and likeness. If it was so, I'm sure the world would have been erased a long time ago or no one would even find answers to their prayers nor would Jesus Christ have been sent to the world to bring us back to redemption. Don't forget, He is a supreme being, and whatever is supreme is far more than human imagination and natural philosophy. He has always been God and will forever be. If God created us, then it means He knows us far more than we know ourselves. What most of us don't understand is that our belief shouldn't only be limited to the fact that "Jesus is

Lord". If God created us in His own image and we also have His spirit in us, then why don't we seek God's opinion about the situation of our lives. Why don't we ask God for direction instead of just complaining and blaming God. I'm not saying that we shouldn't pray for things to happen in our lives (that's necessary). All I'm saying is that when we've prayed and things still don't get to change, why don't we ask God why is it the way it is and not the way we want it and I think **Isaiah 55: 8-9** is the best answer to that.

He knows the best for us. The best for us might not be His best for us. There's always a reason behind every single act of God. Sometimes He might delay it because the time has not yet come; you might abuse it if he gives it to you now. Remember there is time for everything. Many Christians today have turned their backs against God because of lack of understanding. You just missed an appointment for a job interview that you have been praying for (a very long time), you should ask yourself why and not blame God. Sometimes it could be as a result of your own ignorance. He might delay it maybe because something is about to happen. You might eventually pass the interview, but end up as a dead man the next day you're to start the job. In fact, something might be going on in the interview room that God doesn't want you to experience.

> *God allows something to happen in order to save a lot of things from taking place. Just be calm and*

patient because God is good and whatever He does is good.

Funnily enough, we think that our complaint moves God. Let me tell you something, it doesn't change God's personality. He is the same yesterday, today, tomorrow and forevermore. It would only change you and not God. What we think is an act of wickedness might be God's way of securing your tomorrow.

The first instance is from a movie titled God's not dead. This story features a young student who has an argument with his philosophy professor who said God is dead. The movie showed a particular pastor who had been trying to attend a particular event, but couldn't use his own car because it turned faulty on his way to the event. So he had to wait along with his friend. He ordered different cars to drive to the event, but it all became faulty once he started it. He never knew God was delaying his trip to the worship center event so that He would be able to meet with the philosophy professor who was at the point of death.

Story line: The professor believed that God is not real and that He is dead according to his philosophical belief. Due to his position as a professor, he was able to impose that same belief on his students. At the time freshmen students started their first semester course, the professor said to his students during one of his classes he asked his students to tear a paper and wore this inscription on it - "God is Dead", and that whosoever doesn't write it down, he would fail such a person. All did except a guy who wasn't convinced by his professor's words. He tried all he could to prove to the professor that God is Real and Alive, neglecting his grades.

He was also heading to the worship center at the same time the pastor's car started working again. Just at the perfect time when he was hit by a truck, the pastor and his friend arrived at the scene of the accident. Right there, he gave his life to Christ and also gave up the ghost. Can you imagine what would have happened if the pastor had tried all means to attend the event earlier. The professor would have missed it. The pastor kept on worrying about the event and unknown to him, God was preparing the professor for a lifetime encounter through him.

Most times, our blessings come in disguise, but because of a lack of understanding, man begins to blame God. The Bible says that, my people are destroyed because they lack the understanding of the personality of God (paraphrased).

The second instance is that of my admission. I had always wanted to study in the US, but all seemed not to be working. I could have attended the Indian school and still not achieve my goals. Moreover, I could have even written the standardized tests and still end up failing. All I did was to ask God What He was trying to say to me through the problems I was encountering.

We experience problems because they are meant to be solved. And to God be the glory, I was accepted into more than twenty-five schools within a year without a standardized test or an international examination. And right now, I'm on my way to better days; aligning with God's plan and will for my life.

Kindly know that when the purpose of a thing is not known, abuse is inevitable. When you don't know the purpose of God's act over your life, abuse is inevitable, likewise your forward movement also stops.

How do we get to understand the personality of God?

1. Deliberate and consistent study of the Word of God accompanied with daily meditation.
2. Through effective prayer (Pray without ceasing).
3. Through discipline.
4. Have a firm relationship with God.
5. Obedience to the word of God; and
6. Lastly, crave for it. It is the craving that makes you determined and committed to other things expected of you as a child of God

"Understanding God's personality is not a day's work. It requires you to build a genuine love (for God) and relationship with God."

Chapter Seven

The Power Of Words Of Affirmation And Positive Thinking

Many have lost their lives because of negative thinking, and approach towards an event. There's a need to always be positive. You need to, I need to and likewise every other person. We all need to stay positive at all times so as to access the big picture.

A friend of mine would always consider the positive aspect of a thing rather than focusing on the negative part as far as it would benefit her. Adebayo Adewunmi would always say to me, 'Fr I don't like it when people tell me I can't get something as long as it would benefit me". Basically she loves reading a lot, most especially things related to the study of human biology, behavior, and anatomy. She doesn't mind buying a book or a novel for ten thousand naira as far as she's interested in getting to know what its content is all about and what it would eventually offer to her.

This optimistic nature of hers is one basically one of the reasons behind her success as a young teenager. Adewunmi started graphic design, digital marketing, Amazon KDP writing and affiliate marketing at a very young age. Aside from that, she has also completed a diploma in Communication Psychology. At age sixteen, she became a coach and also a mentor in affiliate marketing business.

> **Don't say it won't work out for you. It will.....it's because you don't believe you would make it, that's why it hasn't been working out for you. – Adebayo Adewunmi**

It's not as if she doesn't experience negative turn outs, but she will always put herself on the positive.

Our thoughts define who we are. As a man thinketh in his heart, so is he. Our inward appearance determines our outward expression. Positive thinking produces positive expressions in our lives and negative thoughts produces negativities in our lives. You don't reap what you haven't sowed. You harvest will only be bountiful if you think it will be. This is where faith comes in. A positive mentality helps to build our faith level.

Few months ago, my family and I were privileged to visit a famous tourist center in Abeokuta known as Olumo Rock. We had a photographer with us who led us through the whole place - ascending and descending on the rock. While we were walking, he explained the history behind every nature or artistic work we saw there. When we got to where the people of Egba hid during the war period, he told us the rock is an igneous rock which has a lot of water in it. He explained further that while the Egba people hid in between the rock, whenever rain fell, water dropped from the rock, but at that time it looked like a mystery to them due to the fact that they had no understanding about science. These native people believed the water could heal them and so it did. Whenever anyone fell sick among them, they would drink the water and it did work out for them.

This is the mystery behind positive thinking. What happened to the Egba people does not in any way relate to their spiritual or diabolic nature. All they did was believe that the water would heal them and it did. There's nothing you set your mind to that won't yield results as far as you are very optimistic about it.

Positivity yields productivity while negativity yields negations. Our thoughts have a very significant effect in our lives; it determines our future achievement. If you think the best thing you would ever get is disappointment, then it will, and if you also think the best grade you would ever earn is a B, so will it be. Likewise, if you believe you can get A's in your examinations, surely you would have it that same way.

The same goes with my mentor who always believes that no matter what happens to you in life, God is still cooking better things to come. Most people are not rich because they believe they can never be rich.

Whatever you think and believe is what you will get. I've always had the mentality that I would study outside Nigeria. What you believe is what you would see. You can't plant rice and expect that you would harvest corn. It is impossible. You'll reap whatever you sow.

I remember a time someone asked me what I want to become? I replied…Neurosurgeon. He told me ***"do you wish to spend all the days of your life in the mortuary, experimenting and studying the brain of the dead or don't you know that's what you're going to do?"***. Then I answered him and said ***"I know and that's what I want because that part you just mentioned is the exact thing I love doing"***. Sometimes my colleagues would say to me: so you mean you want to spend sixteen years of your life studying in school to be a licensed Neurosurgeon, no that's much. But do know you what? I'm not concerned about all those things because that's the sacrifice I have to make. I know where I'm heading and what it takes to get there. So, I'm ready to pay the price. It's normal for us to experience challenges, but it is abnormal to accept it as a normal way of life. Always have a positive mindset about things as far as you need to have them or go through them to get to your desired destination. If you're the type that always procrastinates, you're on the wrong track. One thing my humble friend does complain about is people's inability to opt in at good opportunities when it shows up due to the fact that they're always on the negative side.

It's not good enough to be affirmative alone without having a positive mentality and putting it to work as well. **Let's see Adebayo Adewunmi's perspective about words of affirmation and positive thinking.**

> **Some people don't understand that there's a clear line of difference between words of affirmation and positive thinking. I can wake up every morning to tell myself I want to be great. Saying it repeatedly; that's a word of affirmation. You're speaking into your life, future and finance. But listen, you're only speaking because that's what the mouth is meant to do.**
>
> **The difference between words of affirmation and positive thinking is you taking action and having faith. Faith is the substance of things hoped for, the evidence of things not seen(Heb 22:1). Also faith without work is dead. We need to understand this. It's not just you telling**

yourself "I will be great". That's fine, but what do you want to use to be great?.... Nothing. The thing is if people don't Understand the principle of positivity and words of affirmation, they would misplace the two for each other.

A young lady once told me that her words of affirmation are "I will make money". I seemed to like that because the affirmation was strong, but she hasn't been able to achieve that in over three months. She told me she has been praying for wealth. I said again, your affirmation is very nice. Eventually she called to inform me that she has not been able to achieve it, so I asked Why? Because personally, business owners do come to me for advice whenever they are experiencing downtime in their businesses. So I asked this lady, what do you do? Nothing, she replied. You mean nothing? I asked. So how do you expect the wealth to come. Do you expect me to just come to your house and ask for your account number to send ten thousand naira to you? Surprisingly she said and I put in quotes "Things do happen like that". What?

Words of affirmation do not work without positivity. Words of affirmation are just

words. If you're not positive about it, it's rubbish. You have to be positive in your words of affirmation. Life works in a way that everything we do is controlled by our words. The Earth is listening, the air is listening, the trees are listening, and nature itself is also listening to what we say. If we tell ourselves today, I'm not going to do anything, I want to sleep all through. Your body is going to work in that way, and even though you have something to do, you will still sleep; that's the power of the tongue.

Affirmation are words and until you add positivity to it, it will never yield result. Doing something and believing it would work out it positivity. The power of positivity is very great. You can't just speak into your life and not work towards making those words turn into reality – ADEBAYO ADEWUNMI

Do you want to see results? Then be positive about your words of affirmation.

Chapter Eight

Godly Relationship

The Word of God says, **'Evil Communication corrupts good manners'**. A godly relationship does not only mean having a close relationship with God. Though it is the basis of it all, but let's not forget that you can't say you love God when you actually don't love your neighbors in reality. The Bible says love your neighbor as yourself. You can't say you love Him when you don't love your neighbor who are your brothers and sisters).

The relationship you keep determines the outcome your future and how far you will go in life because influence has a lot to do with your future destination. A good relationship has really benefited me a lot. Relationships took me from being an average student. I'm definitely not talking about undefined relationships which are sometimes ungodly because when the purpose of a thing is not known, abuse is inevitable.

Relationship with God.

This is Paramount. It sets us on the platform of touch not my anointed and do my prophet no harm. **1 Corinthians 2:9 says "What eyes have not seen, nor eyes have heard, nor has it entered into the heart of men, are those things which the Lord has prepared for those who love Him".** Like I said earlier, we must recognize that we can't say we love God when we live in hatred with our fellow brethren. Secondly, we must understand that the altar of prayer connects us to the Father more than any other thing. And until God recognizes you, your future is unsecured.

Relationship with Neighbors

Love your neighbor as yourself. I would say again: you can only prove your love for God when you love His people. Don't be a coward, be nice. **See Mark 10:27; 1 Corinthians 1 – 2; 1 Corinthians 13:13; John 4:19 – 21.**

Relationship with Parents.

Honor your father and your mother so that it may be well with you and that you may live long. Your parents are God's representatives on earth to be your caretaker. Whatever you do to your parents determines what will be done to you by the time you have your own children. Your father and mother will always be your parents no matter the circumstances.

Relationship with Friends.

A good relationship breeds good manners while evil communication corrupts good manners. You're meant to influence your friends positively. The friends you keep determines the values you have. It's not necessary that you have a lot of friends. A friend alone can have more impact in your life than having a lot. Before and at the beginning of the year 2023, one major thing I prayed for was a godly relationship. I told God I wanted friends who will help me get to where He has purpose for me. And to God be the glory, their presence is evident in my life today. However, don't let your friends choose you, you're meant to choose them and when you're choosing, choose right. Ask for the help of the Holy Spirit.

Relationship with Mentor

A mentor is a guardian designed to guide you through the journey of life. You need a guardian to be guided in life. A mentor can also be an instructor who is meant to help guide you through achieving your goals in life by making you understand how the world really works. Someone who would tell you how it does work, how to work it out, why it does and doesn't work that way.

I didn't pick my mentor based on spirituality alone. I chose him because he does have what it takes for me to achieve what God has purposed for me. I knew I would not only be spiritual by choosing him, but also a responsible person.

A mentor must be someone you can emulate. I don't suggest people picking their parents as mentors because a mentor is a person who you can share your deepest secret with. Someone who is ready to listen to you, encourage you, and also help you out. Moreover, don't have the mentality that your mentor won't scold you whenever you do misbehave. He would, but in an orderly manner. He would also let you know he understands how you're feeling. Don't try to choose your mentor based on spirituality because he might be spiritual and still doesn't have what it takes for you to get there – the big picture. There has to be a tight connection between you both.

You need to be guided in the journey you're either about to or already started. My mentor made me do things that weren't convenient for me. I had to start praying for an hour, read one chapter of the Bible, and also give a report each day. I obeyed not because I had no choice, but because I wanted to make a difference and also impact others. Nothing comes without a cost; you must be ready to pay the price. You also need to have something in common with your mentor. My mentor and I have something in common which is the ability to write: creating writing. We both have the craving to let the world know what we know is right.

Finally, one thing you must watch out for in mentorship is that if you're still the same way you were before you made that person your mentor, then you're on the wrong track. There has to be a change. I knew I had a gift, but he taught me how to make use of it. I wasn't as prayerful and spiritual as I am now before I met him. So, choose right.

FAILURE TODAY IS NOT FAILURE FOR LIFE. WHEN YOU FALL, ALL YOU NEED TO DO IS TO STAND UP AGAIN AND CONTINUE MOVING ON.

WATCH OUT FOR THE BEST! NO MATTER WHAT LIFE DEMANDS FROM YOU, BE READY TO CONTINUE THE RACE(JOURNEY) IRRESPECTIVE OF THE CIRCUMSTANCES AROUND YOU. WATCH OUT FOR THE BEST BECAUSE YOU'RE THE BEST VERSION OF YOURSELF – LAYU FESTUS PRAISE.

9 789373 355269

Printed at Repro India Ltd.